**PERIPHERAl
DIET PLAN**

The Accurate Diet Plan for Peripheral Neuropathy: Nutritious Foods to Enhance Nerve Function

REX LEWIS

Table of Contents

Introduction

Peripheral Neuropathy Is A Disorder Characterized By Damage To The Peripheral Nerves, Which Play A Crucial Role In Transferring Information Between The Central Nervous System (Brain And Spinal Cord) And The Rest Of The Body. Such Damage Can Result In A Range Of Symptoms, Such As Pain, Numbness, Tingling, And Weakness In The Affected Regions.

Although Peripheral Neuropathy Cannot Be Cured, Adhering To A Nutritious And Well-Balanced Diet Can Significantly Contribute To Symptom Management And Enhance Overall Nerve Well-Being. A Peripheral

Neuropathy Diet Is Designed To Supply Vital Nutrients That Promote Nerve Function, Decrease Inflammation, And Control Underlying Disorders That Can Potentially Cause Nerve Damage.

Below Are Few Crucial Factors To Consider When Following A Diet For Peripheral Neuropathy:

• **Optimal Nutrition:** In Order To Maintain Good Health, It Is Crucial To Consume A Diet That Includes A Balanced Combination Of Carbs, Proteins, And Healthy Fats. Consuming A Well-Rounded Diet Is Crucial For Those With Diabetic Neuropathy As It Aids In The Regulation Of Blood Sugar Levels.

- Omega-3 Fatty Acids, Which Are Present In Fatty Fish, Flaxseeds, Chia Seeds, And Walnuts, Contain Anti-Inflammatory Qualities That Can Potentially Decrease Nerve Irritation.

- Sufficient Consumption Of Vitamins And Minerals, Including B Vitamins (Particularly B1, B6, And B12), Vitamin D, And Magnesium, Is Crucial For Maintaining Nerve Function. These Nutrients Are Involved In The Functioning, Healing, And Regeneration Of Nerves.

- **Antioxidants:** Consuming Foods Abundant In Antioxidants, Such As Fruits And Vegetables, Can Aid In Safeguarding Nerves Against Oxidative Stress. Antioxidants Can Be Obtained

From Berries, Citrus Fruits, And Leafy Greens.

• **Regulating Blood Sugar Levels:** It Is Essential For Individuals With Diabetic Neuropathy To Restrict Their Carbohydrate Consumption In Order To Maintain Stable Blood Sugar Levels. This Entails Selecting Intricate Carbs, Closely Controlling Serving Sizes, And Refraining From Consuming Sugary Foods.

• **Restricting Alcohol And Caffeine:** Consuming Excessive Amounts Of Alcohol Might Contribute To Nerve Damage, Hence It Is Recommended To Restrict Alcohol Consumption. The Level Of Sensitivity To Caffeine Varies Among Individuals, However, Some

Persons May Discover That Lowering Or Completely Eliminating Caffeine From Their Diet Might Help Reduce Symptoms.

Hydration Is Crucial For Maintaining Good Health And Can Potentially Prevent Difficulties Related To Neuropathy, Such As Nerve Damage Caused By Dehydration.

It Is Important To Acknowledge That People May Have Different Reactions To Dietary Changes, Thus It Is Advisable To Seek Guidance From A Healthcare Practitioner Or A Qualified Dietitian To Customize Nutritional Advice Based On Individual Needs And Situations. Moreover, It Is Essential To Address The Root Causes Of

Peripheral Neuropathy, Such As Diabetes Or Autoimmune Illnesses, In Order To Effectively Manage The Condition.

CHAPTER ONE
Basics of Peripheral Neuropathy

Peripheral Neuropathy Is A Disorder Marked By Damage To The Peripheral Nerves, Which Convey Information Between The Central Nervous System (Brain And Spinal Cord) And The Rest Of The Body. These Nerves Regulate A Range Of Functions, Such As Voluntary Muscle Movements, Sensory Perception, And Automatic Bodily Processes. Here Are Some Fundamental Aspects Of Peripheral Neuropathy:

1. Etiology: Peripheral Neuropathy Can Arise From A Multitude Of Factors. Common Reasons Contributing To The Condition Include

Diabetes, Infections (Such As Shingles Or Lyme Disease), Autoimmune Illnesses, Specific Medications (Such As Chemotherapy Treatments Or Certain Antibiotics), Traumatic Injuries, Alcohol Misuse, And Genetic Factors. Occasionally, The Underlying Cause Of The Condition May Be Unidentified (Referred To As Idiopathic Neuropathy).

2. Peripheral Neuropathy Can Be Categorized Into Various Categories, Which Are Determined By The Specific Nerves That Are Impacted And The Corresponding Symptoms That Are Observed. Typical Categories Comprise Sensory Neuropathy (Impairing Sensation), Motor

Neuropathy (Impairing Movement), Autonomic Neuropathy (Impairing Automatic Functions Such As Blood Pressure And Digestion), And Mononeuropathy (Impairing A Single Nerve).

3. Symptoms: Peripheral Neuropathy Can Exhibit A Diverse Range Of Symptoms, Commonly Including:

• **Numbness Or Tingling:** A Prevalent Initial Symptom.

• **Pain:** Characterized By Acute, Piercing, Or Scorching Feelings.

Muscle Weakness Refers To A Lack Of Strength In The Muscles, Which Can Result In Difficulties With Coordination And Balance.

- **Sensitivity:** Increased Responsiveness To Tactile Or Thermal Stimuli.

- **Loss Of Reflexes**: Reflexes May Be Reduced Or Completely Absent.

Changes In Skin, Hair, And Nails May Manifest As Dryness, Hair Loss, And Alterations In The Texture Of Nails And Skin.

4. Diagnosis: Diagnosis Includes A Comprehensive Assessment Of The Patient's Medical History, A Complete Physical Examination, And The Administration Of Numerous Tests. Nerve Conduction Investigations And Electromyography (EMG) Can Assist In Assessing The Magnitude And Nature

Of Nerve Impairment. Underlying Reasons, Such As Diabetes Or Vitamin Deficiencies, Can Be Identified Through Blood Tests.

5. Treatment: Peripheral Neuropathy Is An Incurable Condition, However Management Options Focus On Relieving Symptoms And Addressing The Root Cause. Possible Interventions May Encompass:

• Medications Such As Analgesics, Anticonvulsants, And Antidepressants May Be Recommended.

• Physical Therapy Involves Performing Exercises That Aim To Enhance Muscle Strength, Coordination, And Balance.

• Occupational Therapy Involves Aiding Individuals In Their Regular Duties And Enhancing Their Overall Functioning.

• Managing Underlying Conditions Involves The Treatment Of Medical Diseases Such As Diabetes Or Infections.

Pain Management Techniques Such As Heat Therapy, Cold Packs, And Transcutaneous Electrical Nerve Stimulation (TENS) Can Be Effective.

6. **Prevention:** Certain Types Of Peripheral Neuropathy Can Be Averted By Effectively Controlling Underlying Health Disorders, Abstaining From Excessive Alcohol

Use, Upholding A Healthy Lifestyle, And Swiftly Addressing Injuries.

It Is Crucial For Persons Who Are Suffering Symptoms Of Peripheral Neuropathy To Promptly Seek Medical Assistance In Order To Receive An Accurate Diagnosis And Appropriate Treatment. Timely Management Can Mitigate Additional Nerve Damage And Enhance Overall Quality Of Life.

How Diet Impacts Neuropathy

The Effect Of Diet In Influencing Neuropathy, Particularly In Situations Such As Diabetic Neuropathy Where Blood Sugar Levels Are A Critical Determinant, Is Of Utmost Importance. There Are Multiple Ways In Which Nutrition Might Impact Neuropathy:

- **Blood Sugar Regulation:** It Is Crucial For Patients With Diabetes To Maintain Stable Blood Sugar Levels In Order To Avoid And Manage Diabetic Neuropathy. Prolonged Elevation Of Blood Glucose Levels Can Result In Progressive Nerve Injury. An Eating Plan That Prioritizes Complex Carbohydrates, Foods High In Fiber, And Carefully Measured Serving Sizes Can Effectively Regulate Blood Glucose Levels.

- **Nutrient Deficiencies:** Specific Vitamins And Minerals Are Crucial For Maintaining Optimal Nerve Health. Neuropathy Has Been Associated With Insufficiencies Of B Vitamins (B1, B6, B12), Vitamin D, And Magnesium.

Incorporating A Diverse Range Of Fruits, Vegetables, Whole Grains, And Lean Proteins Into Your Diet Helps Supply You With These Vital Nutrients.

• Consuming Anti-Inflammatory Foods Can Potentially Help Reduce Nerve Damage Caused By Chronic Inflammation In Neuropathy. Consuming Foods That Provide Anti-Inflammatory Characteristics, Such As Fatty Fish (Rich In Omega-3 Fatty Acids), Nuts, Seeds, And Vibrant Fruits And Vegetables, Can Potentially Diminish Inflammation And Promote The Well-Being Of Nerves.

• Omega-3 Fatty Acids, Which May Be Found In Fish, Flaxseeds, And Walnuts, Possess Anti-Inflammatory Properties

And May Aid In Protecting Nerves. Incorporating These Sources Of Nutritious Fats Into One's Diet Can Have Advantageous Effects.

- It Is Advisable To Minimize Or Abstain From Alcohol Consumption Since It Can Potentially Lead To Nerve Damage. Moreover, Specific Medications Or Substances Might Potentially Cause Harm To The Nervous System, Hence It Is Crucial To Adhere To Medical Guidance And Refrain From Using Chemicals That Could Exacerbate Neuropathy.

- Hydration Is Important As Dehydration Can Worsen Symptoms Of Neuropathy. Ensuring Adequate Hydration Is Crucial For Overall Well-

Being And Can Aid In The Prevention Of Issues Linked To Nerve Injury.

- **Prudent Attitude Towards Caffeine:** Although The Connection Between Caffeine And Neuropathy Is Not Definitively Proven, Certain Individuals May Discover That Lowering Or Completely Eliminating Caffeine Can Assist In Alleviating Symptoms. It Is Recommended To Carefully Study One's Personal Reactions To Caffeine And Make Appropriate Modifications.

- **Weight Management:** It Is Crucial To Maintain A Healthy Weight, Particularly For Persons Who Have Diabetes. Insulin Resistance And Diabetic Neuropathy Can Be

Exacerbated By Obesity And Excessive Body Weight. Adhering To A Well-Rounded Diet Along With Consistent Physical Exercise Can Assist In The Control And Maintenance Of Body Weight.

It Is Important To Acknowledge That People May Have Different Reactions To Dietary Modifications, And Recommendations Should Be Tailored To The Specific Type And Cause Of Neuropathy. Seeking Guidance From A Healthcare Expert Or A Registered Dietitian Is Essential For Developing A Personalized Dietary Plan That Aligns With An Individual's Specific Needs And Health Circumstances. Furthermore, It Is Crucial To Address

The Root Causes Of Neuropathy As A Fundamental Aspect Of Holistic Care.

CHAPTER TWO
Essential Nutrients for Nerve Health

Nerve health is closely linked to the intake of certain essential nutrients that play vital roles in nerve function, repair, and overall well-being. Here are some key nutrients that are crucial for maintaining and supporting nerve health:

B Vitamins:

- **B1 (Thiamine):** Essential for nerve function and carbohydrate metabolism. Sources include whole grains, nuts, seeds, and legumes.
- **B6 (Pyridoxine):** Necessary for the synthesis of

neurotransmitters. Found in poultry, fish, bananas, and potatoes.

- **B12 (Cobalamin):** Important for nerve cell maintenance and myelin production. Found in meat, fish, dairy products, and fortified foods.

Vitamin D:

- **Role:** Plays a role in nerve function, and deficiency may be associated with neuropathy.
- **Sources:** Sunlight exposure, fatty fish (salmon, mackerel), fortified dairy products, and supplements if necessary.

Vitamin E:

- **Role:** Acts as an antioxidant, protecting nerve cells from oxidative damage.
- **Sources:** Nuts, seeds, spinach, and vegetable oils.

Omega-3 Fatty Acids:

- **Role:** Have anti-inflammatory properties, important for nerve health.
- **Sources:** Fatty fish (salmon, mackerel, sardines), flaxseeds, chia seeds, and walnuts.

Magnesium:

- **Role:** Supports nerve function, muscle contraction, and relaxation.

- **Sources:** Leafy green vegetables, nuts, seeds, whole grains, and legumes.

Calcium:

- **Role:** Essential for nerve impulse transmission and muscle function.
- **Sources:** Dairy products, leafy greens, fortified plant-based milk, and supplements if necessary.

Antioxidants:

- **Role:** Protect nerves from oxidative stress and inflammation.
- **Sources:** Colorful fruits and vegetables (berries, oranges,

bell peppers), green tea, and dark chocolate.

Iron:

- **Role:** Supports oxygen transport and energy production in nerve cells.
- **Sources:** Lean meats, poultry, fish, legumes, and fortified cereals.

Zinc:

- **Role:** Important for nerve signaling and function.
- **Sources:** Meat, dairy, nuts, seeds, and whole grains.

Coenzyme Q10 (CoQ10):

- **Role:** An antioxidant that supports cellular energy production.
- **Sources:** Fish, meat, nuts, and seeds.

It's important to note that obtaining these nutrients through a well-balanced diet is generally the best approach. However, in some cases, supplements may be recommended if there are deficiencies or challenges in meeting nutritional needs through food alone. Before making significant changes to your diet or taking supplements, it's advisable to consult with a healthcare professional or a registered dietitian to ensure that the approach is personalized and safe based on individual health conditions and requirements.

Analyzing the concepts of inflammation and neuropathy

Inflammation is an intricate physiological reaction initiated by the immune system in reaction to detrimental stimuli, such as viruses, injury, or damaged cells. Inflammation is a necessary and inherent aspect of the body's immune response, but when it becomes chronic or protracted, it can contribute to a range of health issues, including neuropathy.

To comprehend the connection between inflammation and neuropathy, it is crucial to acknowledge how inflammation can cause nerve injury and affect the development of neuropathic disorders. Below are few crucial factors to take into account:

• **Inflammatory Neuropathy**: Certain neuropathic diseases exhibit an inflammatory aspect, such as autoimmune neuropathies. Conditions such as Guillain-Barré syndrome are characterized by the immune system's assault on the peripheral nerves, resulting in inflammation and harm.

• **Oxidative Stress:** Inflammation has the potential to produce reactive oxygen species, also known as free radicals, which can lead to oxidative stress. Oxidative stress has the potential to harm cells, particularly nerve cells, and play a role in the advancement of neuropathy.

• **Nerve Compression:** Inflammation can cause edema and subsequent compression of nerves in specific medical circumstances. Conditions such as carpal tunnel syndrome are characterized by inflammation and compression of the median nerve in the wrist, resulting in symptoms such as numbness and tingling in the hands.

• **Underlying Health Disorders:** Chronic inflammatory disorders, such as rheumatoid arthritis or lupus, can potentially lead to the development of neuropathy. In such instances, the inflammation linked to the underlying illness can impact the nerves.

• **Diabetes and Inflammation:** Diabetes is a prevalent factor in the occurrence of neuropathy, and inflammation is a contributing factor in the progression of diabetic neuropathy. Diabetes can cause prolonged elevation in blood sugar levels, which can result in inflammation and harm to the blood vessels that provide nerves.

• **Immune System Modulation:** modulating the immune system can be used as a therapeutic method to manage neuropathy in some circumstances. Immunosuppressive drugs can be employed to diminish inflammation and decelerate the advancement of some autoimmune neuropathies.

• **The Relationship Between Diet and Inflammation:** Consuming a diet that is abundant in foods with anti-inflammatory properties, such as fruits, vegetables, fatty fish, and nuts, can potentially reduce inflammation and promote the well-being of nerves. Conversely, a diet that contains a significant amount of processed foods and saturated fats can potentially lead to inflammation.

• **Pain and Inflammation:** Inflammation can exacerbate pain in neuropathy. Addressing inflammation can be a key component of a comprehensive pain management strategy for those suffering from neuropathic pain.

It is crucial to acknowledge that although inflammation plays a role in certain forms of neuropathy, it may not be the predominant cause in other instances. Neuropathy can be attributed to a range of different causes, and it is essential to identify and address the exact cause in order to effectively manage the condition. Individuals exhibiting signs of neuropathy should promptly consult a medical professional for an accurate diagnosis and suitable therapy.

CHAPTER THREE
Connection between Diabetes and Neuropathy

The connection between diabetes and neuropathy is well-established, and diabetes is one of the most common causes of neuropathy. Neuropathy in the context of diabetes is often referred to as diabetic neuropathy. The relationship between diabetes and neuropathy involves several factors:

1. **High Blood Sugar Levels (Hyperglycemia):**
    - ➢ Prolonged high levels of glucose in the blood, a condition known as hyperglycemia, can lead to nerve damage.

Elevated blood sugar levels contribute to chemical changes in the nerves that impair their ability to transmit signals.

2. **Vascular Damage:**

   ➢ Diabetes can lead to damage to blood vessels, reducing blood flow to nerves. The compromised blood supply deprives nerves of essential nutrients and oxygen, contributing to nerve damage.

3. **Advanced Glycation End Products (AGEs):**

   ➢ High blood sugar can result in the formation of

advanced glycation end products (AGEs). These substances can accumulate in nerve tissues, leading to inflammation and damage.

4. **Autoimmune Factors:**

   ➤ In some cases, diabetes may have autoimmune components, where the immune system mistakenly attacks and damages nerve cells. This autoimmune response can contribute to inflammation and nerve damage.

5. **Poorly Controlled Diabetes:**

> The risk of neuropathy is higher in individuals with poorly controlled diabetes. Consistently managing blood sugar levels within the target range is crucial in preventing or slowing the progression of diabetic neuropathy.

6. **Types of Diabetic Neuropathy:**

> There are different types of diabetic neuropathy, each affecting specific nerves and presenting with distinct symptoms. These include peripheral neuropathy (affecting the

extremities), autonomic neuropathy (affecting involuntary functions like digestion and heart rate), proximal neuropathy (affecting thighs, hips, or buttocks), and focal neuropathy (affecting specific nerves).

7. **Risk Factors:**

> Various factors increase the risk of diabetic neuropathy, including the duration of diabetes, poor blood sugar control, smoking, high blood pressure, and genetics.

8. **Symptoms:**

> Diabetic neuropathy can manifest with symptoms such as tingling, numbness, burning sensations, and pain in the affected areas. Muscle weakness and problems with coordination may also occur.

9. **Prevention and Management:**

> Proper management of diabetes, including medication, lifestyle modifications (such as a balanced diet and regular exercise), and regular monitoring of blood sugar levels, is crucial in preventing or slowing the

progression of diabetic neuropathy.

It's important for individuals with diabetes to be proactive in managing their condition to reduce the risk of neuropathy and its complications. Regular check-ups with healthcare providers, including monitoring for early signs of neuropathy, can aid in early detection and intervention. Controlling blood sugar levels and adopting a healthy lifestyle are key components in the prevention and management of diabetic neuropathy.

Importance of Omega-3s for Nerve Health

Omega-3 fatty acids, particularly EPA (eicosapentaenoic acid) and DHA (docosahexaenoic acid), are essential polyunsaturated fats with numerous health benefits, including significant importance for nerve health. Here are several reasons why omega-3s are considered crucial for maintaining and supporting nerve health:

Anti-Inflammatory Properties:

• Omega-3 fatty acids are well-known for their anti-inflammatory effects. Chronic inflammation can contribute to nerve damage and various neurological disorders. By reducing inflammation, omega-3s may help protect nerves from damage and support their proper function.

Myelin Formation and Maintenance:

• Myelin is a protective sheath that covers nerve fibers, facilitating efficient transmission of nerve signals. DHA, a component of omega-3 fatty acids, is a crucial structural element of myelin. Adequate levels of DHA support the formation and maintenance of myelin, promoting optimal nerve conduction.

Neurotransmitter Function:

• Omega-3 fatty acids play a role in neurotransmitter function. They contribute to the fluidity and function of cell membranes, including those of nerve cells. This can influence the release and reception of neurotransmitters, the chemical messengers that facilitate communication between nerve cells.

Neuroprotection and Antioxidant Effects:

• Omega-3s possess neuroprotective properties and may act as antioxidants, helping to combat oxidative stress in nerve cells. Oxidative stress can lead to cellular damage, and by reducing it, omega-3s contribute to overall nerve health.

Antiplatelet Effects:

• Omega-3 fatty acids have mild antiplatelet effects, meaning they can help prevent excessive blood clotting. This is relevant to nerve health as adequate blood flow is crucial for delivering oxygen and nutrients to nerves, supporting their function and preventing ischemic damage.

Mood and Cognitive Function:

• Omega-3 fatty acids are associated with improved mood and cognitive function. While the exact mechanisms are not fully understood, omega-3s are believed to influence neurotransmitter function and may contribute to the overall well-being of the nervous system.

Reducing Neuropathic Pain:

• Some studies suggest that omega-3 supplementation may help reduce neuropathic pain, a common symptom in various neuropathic conditions. The anti-inflammatory and neuroprotective effects of omega-3s may play a role in alleviating pain associated with nerve damage.

Sources of Omega-3 Fatty Acids:

• Fatty fish (such as salmon, mackerel, and sardines), flaxseeds, chia seeds, walnuts, and algae-based supplements are excellent sources of omega-3 fatty acids.

While omega-3 fatty acids offer numerous benefits for nerve health, it's important to maintain a balanced diet that includes a variety of nutrients. Before considering supplementation, individuals should consult with healthcare professionals, especially if they have existing medical conditions or take medications, to ensure that omega-3 supplementation is safe and appropriate for their individual needs.

CHAPTER FOUR
Preventing the Use of Toxic Substances

It is imperative to abstain from noxious chemicals in order to sustain general health and well-being, which includes the well-being of the neurological system. Toxic substances can lead to a range of health issues, such as nerve damage and the development or worsening of neuropathy. Here are some crucial items to refrain from or consume in moderation to promote nerve health:

1. Excessive Alcohol: Consuming large amounts of alcohol can cause damage to the nervous system and result in alcoholic neuropathy.

Abstaining from or minimizing alcohol consumption is beneficial for safeguarding the integrity of the neurological system.

2. Tobacco Smoke: Smoking subjects the body to noxious substances that might injure blood vessels and diminish blood circulation to nerves. Cessation of smoking is necessary for optimal physical well-being and proper functioning of the nervous system.

3. Illicit Drugs: The consumption of specific illicit substances might cause harmful consequences to the nervous system. Substances such as cocaine, methamphetamines, and opioids have the potential to contribute to neuropathy and other neurological disorders.

4. Certain drugs: when used improperly or excessively, can cause damage to the nervous system. It is imperative to adhere to specified medication regimens and seek guidance from healthcare specialists regarding potential adverse effects.

5. Consuming diets that are rich in processed foods and trans fats might potentially lead to inflammation and oxidative stress, which can have detrimental effects on the health of nerves. It is advisable to follow a diet that includes a variety of whole foods, fruits, vegetables, and healthy fats.

6. Excessive caffeine use can lead to anxiety, sleep difficulties, and worsen neuropathic symptoms in persons who are sensitive to it. Although moderate caffeine intake is generally safe for most people, consuming too much can have negative effects. It is recommended to closely observe one's individual tolerance to caffeine.

7. Environmental Toxins: Exposure to specific environmental toxins, such as heavy metals (lead, mercury), pesticides, and industrial chemicals, might contribute to the occurrence of nerve injury. Implementing safety precautions and opting for organic produce can have advantageous effects by reducing one's exposure to potential harm.

8. Consuming processed sugar and high-glycemic foods can lead to inflammation and worsen problems such as diabetic neuropathy. It is crucial to maintain stable blood sugar levels by following a well-balanced diet.

9. Artificial Sweeteners: Certain research indicates a possible correlation between artificial sweeteners and neurological disorders. Although further research is necessary, opting for natural sweeteners in moderation may be a wise decision.

10. Elevated Sodium Consumption:
Consuming an excessive amount of salt can contribute to hypertension, which can have a negative impact on the blood vessels that provide nourishment to the neurons. It is crucial to adhere to a diet that is both balanced and low in sodium.

There is variation in how individuals react to substances, therefore it is crucial to take into account unique health circumstances and seek guidance from healthcare professionals for tailored recommendations. Adopting lifestyle choices that promote general health, such as following a well-balanced diet, engaging in regular physical activity, and abstaining from dangerous substances, can help in keeping a healthy nervous system.

Meal Planning for Neuropathy

Meal Planning For Neuropathy Involves Focusing On A Balanced And Nutritious Diet To Support Overall Health And Provide Essential Nutrients For Nerve Function. Here Are Some General Guidelines For Meal Planning That May Be Beneficial For Individuals With Neuropathy:

1. **Balanced Diet:**
   - Include A Mix Of Carbohydrates, Proteins, And Healthy Fats In Each Meal. This Helps Provide

A Steady Source Of Energy And Supports Various Bodily Functions, Including Nerve Health.

2. **Complex Carbohydrates:**
   - Choose Complex Carbohydrates That Have A Lower Impact On Blood Sugar Levels. Whole Grains, Legumes, Fruits, And Vegetables Are Good Sources Of Complex Carbohydrates.

3. **Lean Proteins:**
   - Include Lean Protein Sources Such As Poultry, Fish, Tofu, Legumes, And Beans. Protein Is Essential For Tissue

Repair And Muscle Function, Which Can Be Important For Those With Neuropathy.

4. **Healthy Fats:**

   - Incorporate Sources Of Healthy Fats, Such As Avocados, Nuts, Seeds, And Olive Oil. Omega-3 Fatty Acids, Found In Fatty Fish Like Salmon, Can Also Be Beneficial For Nerve Health.

5. **Fruits And Vegetables:**

   - Aim For A Variety Of Colorful Fruits And Vegetables To Ensure A Range Of Vitamins, Minerals, And

Antioxidants. These Nutrients Play A Role In Reducing Inflammation And Supporting Overall Health.

6. **B Vitamins:**

   - Include Foods Rich In B Vitamins, As They Are Crucial For Nerve Function. Good Sources Include Whole Grains, Leafy Greens, Nuts, Seeds, And Lean Meats.

7. **Vitamin D:**

   - Include Foods Rich In Vitamin D, Such As Fatty Fish (Salmon, Mackerel), Fortified Dairy Products, And Egg Yolks. Vitamin D

Is Important For Nerve Health And Overall Bone Health.

8. **Magnesium:**

   - Incorporate Magnesium-Rich Foods Like Leafy Green Vegetables, Nuts, Seeds, And Whole Grains. Magnesium Is Involved In Nerve Function And Muscle Contraction.

9. **Hydration:**

   - Stay Well-Hydrated, As Dehydration Can Exacerbate Symptoms Of Neuropathy. Water Is The Best Choice, And Herbal Teas Can Also Contribute To Hydration.

10. **Controlled Portion Sizes:**

- Be Mindful Of Portion Sizes To Help Regulate Blood Sugar Levels, Especially For Individuals With Diabetic Neuropathy. This Can Contribute To Better Glycemic Control.

11. **Limit Processed Foods And Sugar:**

- Minimize The Intake Of Processed Foods, Sugary Snacks, And Beverages. These Can Contribute To Inflammation And May Negatively Impact Nerve Health.

12. **Limit Sodium Intake:**

- Reduce Sodium Intake By Choosing Fresh, Whole Foods Over Processed And Packaged Options. High Sodium Levels Can Affect Blood Pressure And Potentially Impact Nerves.

13. **Consideration Of Food Sensitivities:**

- Some Individuals May Have Food Sensitivities That Can Exacerbate Neuropathic Symptoms. Pay Attention To How Certain Foods Affect Your Symptoms And Consider Consulting With A Healthcare Professional

Or A Registered Dietitian For Personalized Advice.

It's Important To Note That Individual Responses To Dietary Changes May Vary, And Consulting With A Healthcare Professional Or A Registered Dietitian Is Recommended To Tailor Dietary Recommendations To Specific Needs And Conditions. Additionally, Addressing The Underlying Causes Of Neuropathy And Maintaining A Healthy Lifestyle Are Integral Components Of Comprehensive Management.

CHAPTER FIVE
A Synopsis of Dietary Supplements

Nutritional supplements are specifically formulated goods intended to augment the diet and supply vital elements that may be deficient or inadequate in one's typical food consumption. These supplements are available in a variety of formats, such as pills, capsules, powders, liquids, and gummies. It is crucial to acknowledge that although supplements can be advantageous for specific individuals, they cannot replace a well-rounded and diverse diet. Provided is a summary of several prevalent nutritional supplements and their possible advantages:

Multivitamins:

• Multivitamins contain a combination of essential vitamins and minerals. They are designed to fill nutritional gaps in the diet and provide a broad spectrum of nutrients, including vitamin A, B vitamins, vitamin C, vitamin D, vitamin E, and minerals like calcium, magnesium, and zinc.

Omega-3 Fatty Acids:

• Omega-3 supplements, often derived from fish oil or algae, provide essential fatty acids like EPA (eicosapentaenoic acid) and DHA (docosahexaenoic acid). These fatty acids are known for their anti-inflammatory properties and are crucial for heart health, brain function, and nerve health.

Vitamin D:

• Vitamin D supplements are commonly recommended for individuals with limited sun exposure or those at risk of vitamin D deficiency. Vitamin D is essential for bone health, immune function, and may have implications for nerve health.

Calcium and Vitamin D:

• Calcium supplements, often combined with vitamin D, are taken to support bone health. Adequate calcium intake is crucial for preventing conditions like osteoporosis.

Iron:

• Iron supplements are recommended for individuals with iron deficiency anemia. Iron is essential for the production of hemoglobin, the oxygen-carrying component of red blood cells.

B Vitamins:

• B-complex supplements typically include B1 (thiamine), B2 (riboflavin), B3 (niacin), B5 (pantothenic acid), B6 (pyridoxine), B7 (biotin), B9 (folate), and B12 (cobalamin). These vitamins play crucial roles in energy metabolism, nerve function, and red blood cell production.

Magnesium:

• Magnesium supplements are taken to support muscle and nerve function, blood pressure regulation, and bone health. Magnesium is found in various foods, but supplementation may be necessary for some individuals.

Probiotics:

• Probiotics contain live beneficial bacteria that promote a healthy gut microbiome. They are believed to support digestion, immune function, and may have broader implications for overall health.

Antioxidants:

• Antioxidant supplements, including vitamins C and E, selenium, and coenzyme Q10, are taken to neutralize free radicals in the body and reduce oxidative stress.

Glucosamine and Chondroitin:

• These supplements are often used for joint health and may be taken by individuals with osteoarthritis. They are thought to support joint structure and function.

It's important to use nutritional supplements with caution and under the guidance of healthcare professionals, especially for individuals with existing health conditions or those taking medications. Overconsumption of certain vitamins and minerals can have adverse effects, and individual nutritional needs vary. A balanced diet that includes a variety of nutrient-dense foods is generally the best way to meet nutritional requirements. Before starting any supplement regimen, it's advisable to consult with a healthcare provider or a registered dietitian to ensure that the chosen supplements are appropriate for individual health needs.

Why Frequent Exercise Is Important

Consistent physical activity is essential for preserving overall health and well-being. It provides a diverse array of physical, mental, and emotional advantages that have a good influence on different facets of our lives. Here are few crucial factors emphasizing the significance of consistent physical activity:

Cardiovascular Health:

• Regular exercise strengthens the heart, improves circulation, and helps manage blood pressure and cholesterol levels. It reduces the risk of cardiovascular diseases such as heart attacks and strokes.

Weight Management:

• Engaging in regular physical activity helps with weight control by burning calories and increasing metabolism. It plays a significant role in preventing obesity and related health conditions.

Muscle Strength and Flexibility:

• Exercise promotes the development of muscle strength and flexibility. This is essential for maintaining proper posture, preventing injuries, and supporting overall physical function.

Bone Health:

• Weight-bearing exercises, such as walking, running, and resistance training, contribute to bone density and help prevent conditions like osteoporosis. Strong bones are essential for overall mobility and functionality.

Improved Mental Health:

• Exercise has profound effects on mental well-being. It reduces symptoms of depression and anxiety, enhances mood, and promotes relaxation. Regular physical activity has been linked to improved cognitive function and reduced risk of neurodegenerative diseases.

Enhanced Sleep Quality:

• Regular exercise is associated with better sleep quality. It helps regulate sleep patterns, promotes relaxation, and can alleviate symptoms of insomnia.

Boosted Immune System:

• Moderate, regular exercise can strengthen the immune system, making the body more resistant to illnesses and infections.

Improved Metabolic Health:

• Physical activity plays a crucial role in regulating blood sugar levels and improving insulin sensitivity. This is especially important in preventing and managing conditions like type 2 diabetes.

Increased Energy Levels:

• It improves oxygen and nutrient delivery to tissues, helping the cardiovascular and respiratory systems work more efficiently.

Social Interaction:

• Participating in group exercises, sports, or fitness classes provides opportunities for social interaction and community engagement. This contributes to emotional well-being and a sense of belonging.

Stress Management:

• Exercise is an effective stress reliever. Physical activity stimulates the release of endorphins, the body's natural mood lifters, which can help reduce stress and anxiety.

Longevity:

• Numerous studies suggest that regular exercise is associated with increased life expectancy. It promotes a healthier lifestyle and reduces the risk of chronic diseases that can impact longevity.

Disease Prevention:

• Regular physical activity has been linked to a reduced risk of various chronic conditions, including heart disease, certain cancers, and metabolic disorders.

Cognitive Benefits:

• Exercise has been shown to enhance cognitive function, including memory, attention, and learning. It may also reduce the risk of cognitive decline as individuals age.

It's important to note that the type and intensity of exercise can vary based on individual fitness levels, health conditions, and preferences. It's advisable to consult with a healthcare professional before starting a new exercise program, especially for individuals with pre-existing health conditions. Regular exercise, when combined with a healthy diet and lifestyle, is a powerful tool for achieving and maintaining optimal health.

Healthy Recipes for People with Neuropathy

When designing meals suitable for individuals with neuropathy, it is crucial to prioritize foods that are rich in nutrients, have anti-inflammatory properties, and promote nerve health and general well-being. Below are two recipes that have components abundant in vitamins, minerals, and good fats, which might be advantageous for patients with neuropathy:

Recipe 1: Grilled Salmon with Quinoa and Roasted Vegetables

Ingredients:

- 2 salmon fillets
- 1 cup quinoa (uncooked)
- 2 cups mixed vegetables (e.g., bell peppers, zucchini, cherry tomatoes)
- 2 tablespoons olive oil
- 1 teaspoon lemon zest
- 2 tablespoons lemon juice
- 2 cloves garlic, minced
- Fresh herbs (such as parsley or dill), chopped
- Salt and pepper to taste

Instructions:

1. Preheat the oven to 400°F (200°C).

2. Cook quinoa according to package instructions.

3. Toss the mixed vegetables with 1 tablespoon of olive oil, salt, and pepper. Spread them on a baking sheet and roast in the oven for 15-20 minutes or until tender.

4. In a small bowl, mix the remaining olive oil, lemon zest, lemon juice, minced garlic, and chopped herbs to create a dressing.

5. Season the salmon fillets with salt and pepper. Grill or pan-sear the salmon until cooked to your liking.

6. Assemble the meal by placing a serving of quinoa on each plate, topping it with grilled salmon, and serving the roasted vegetables on the side. Drizzle the lemon herb dressing over the entire dish.

Recipe 2: Lentil and Vegetable Soup

Ingredients:

- 1 cup dry green or brown lentils, rinsed
- 1 onion, chopped
- 2 carrots, diced
- 2 celery stalks, chopped
- 3 cloves garlic, minced
- 1 can (14 oz) diced tomatoes
- 6 cups vegetable broth

- 1 teaspoon ground turmeric
- 1 teaspoon ground cumin
- 1 teaspoon paprika
- Salt and pepper to taste
- 2 cups spinach or kale, chopped
- Lemon wedges for serving

Instructions:

1. In a large pot, sauté the chopped onion, carrots, celery, and garlic until softened.
2. Add lentils, diced tomatoes, vegetable broth, turmeric, cumin, paprika, salt, and pepper. Bring to a boil, then reduce heat and simmer for about 20-25 minutes or until lentils are tender.

3. Add chopped spinach or kale to the pot and cook for an additional 5 minutes until the greens are wilted.

4. Adjust seasoning as needed. Serve the soup hot with a squeeze of fresh lemon juice.

These recipes incorporate ingredients rich in omega-3 fatty acids, antioxidants, and anti-inflammatory properties, which are beneficial for supporting nerve health. Remember to tailor these recipes to individual dietary preferences and restrictions, and consult with a healthcare professional or a registered dietitian for personalized advice.

Conclusion

To summarize, the management of neuropathy requires a holistic strategy that encompasses lifestyle decisions, nutritional factors, and consistent physical activity. It is crucial to comprehend the significance of maintaining a well-balanced diet that is abundant in nutrients that promote the health of nerves. Key components include the incorporation of meals with anti-inflammatory properties, ensuring sufficient hydration, and avoiding hazardous substances.

Nutritional supplements can provide advantages, particularly in treating certain insufficiencies, but their usage should be approached with caution and under the supervision of healthcare specialists. Vital nutrients, including B vitamins, omega-3 fatty acids, and antioxidants, are essential for optimal neuron function and overall health.

Consistent physical activity is a fundamental aspect of neuropathy treatment, as it promotes cardiovascular fitness, aids in weight control, enhances mental health, and improves overall quality of life. It enhances blood circulation, diminishes inflammation, and facilitates the body's innate healing mechanisms.

In addition, persons suffering from neuropathy should collaborate closely with healthcare specialists, such as physicians and qualified dietitians, to develop customized strategies that cater to their unique requirements and underlying health concerns. Effective management of neuropathy requires monitoring symptoms, making appropriate modifications to lifestyle and nutritional choices, and obtaining help from healthcare professionals.

Incorporating a comprehensive strategy that integrates a well-rounded lifestyle, appropriate nourishment, and consistent physical activity will ultimately enhance nerve well-being and enhance the overall standard of living for persons experiencing neuropathy.

THE END

Made in United States
Troutdale, OR
12/08/2024

26069109R00050